SOCIAL MEDIA DOMINATION

Master Social Media Marketing Strategies with Facebook, Twitter, YouTube, Instagram and LinkedIn

KENNETH LEWIS

Copyright 2016 by Kenneth Lewis - All rights reserved.

This document is geared towards providing exact and reliable information in regards to the topic and issue covered. The publication is sold with the idea that the publisher is not required to render accounting, officially permitted, or otherwise, qualified services. If advice is necessary, legal or professional, a practiced individual in the profession should be ordered.

From a Declaration of Principles which was accepted and approved equally by a Committee of the American Bar Association and a Committee of Publishers and Associations.

In no way is it legal to reproduce, duplicate, or transmit any part of this document in either electronic means or in printed format. Recording of this publication is strictly prohibited and any storage of this document is not allowed unless with written permission from the publisher. All rights reserved.

The information provided herein is stated to be truthful and consistent, in that any liability, in terms of inattention or otherwise, by any usage or abuse of any policies, processes, or directions contained within is the solitary and utter responsibility of the recipient reader. Under no circumstances will any legal responsibility or blame be held against the publisher for any reparation, damages, or monetary loss due to the information herein, either directly or indirectly.

Respective authors own all copyrights not held by the publisher.

The information herein is offered for informational purposes solely, and is universal as so. The presentation of the information is without contract or any type of guarantee assurance.

The trademarks that are used are without any consent, and the publication of the trademark is without permission or backing by the trademark owner. All trademarks and brands within this book are for clarifying purposes only and are the owned by the owners themselves, not affiliated with this document.

ISBN: 1523353473
ISBN-13: 978-1523353477

DEDICATED TO
THE READER

May you achieve success in all your business
and entrepreneurial endeavors.

TABLE OF CONTENTS

i	Introduction	1
1	Social Media Advice	7
2	Facebook	17
3	Twitter	23
4	YouTube	31
5	Instagram	37
6	LinkedIn	43
7	Resources Discussed	51
ii	Conclusion	57
iii	Bonus Excerpt of *Facebook Marketing: How to Use Facebook for Effective Internet Marketing and Social Media Success*	67
iv	Other Works by Kenneth Lewis	77
v	About the Author	81

INTRODUCTION

I want to congratulate you on taking the initiative to bring your product or business to the next level by reading this book.

This book contains proven steps and strategies on how to take advantage of the nascent phenomenon that is social media. For those of us who are not rabid socialites, when confronted with the widespread social media usage we often find ourselves a little overwhelmed at just how far these websites and apps have penetrated everyday life. This is especially true for contemporary business owners who now need to capitalize on multiple mediums of social media or risk fading into irrelevancy.

Nowadays it is not enough to just be savvy with the internet, using the tried and true marketing techniques employed in that realm. Now if you want the best chances at reaching your audience, social media is your best ally, regardless of whether you want it to be.

To add to this challenge, the way companies use social media is inherently different from the way companies have advertised previously. Even if you learn the ropes of how to use your chosen social media platforms. You need to learn how to build a relationship with your customers and build a loyal and consistent following by providing value to others. You need to learn how to not simply bombard your followers with blatant advertisement, but invite them to enjoy your brand by producing high quality content for their feeds.

This book exists as a guide to help any business owner familiarize themselves with five of the largest social media platforms: Facebook, Twitter, YouTube, Instagram and LinkedIn. We will start in the shallow waters, exploring the purpose of each of these specific platforms and how they are used. We will explore the importance of interconnectivity, how to produce high quality content, how to effectively create a brand and where to find the various tools that exist to boost your efforts.

We will discuss how to use the unique features of each platform to our advantage, tailoring our content and branding for the greatest success. The respective sections delve into the five before mentioned social media websites and how to master them. Be taught the essentials between major platforms like Twitter and Facebook, the importance of these differences and how to wisely customize your campaign to optimize your marketing efforts.

Finally, take your business or product to the new level

by expanding your knowledge of the Facebook platform to even greater depths by learning advanced strategies in *Facebook Marketing: How to Use Facebook for Effective Internet Marketing and Social Media Success* in our bonus excerpt section.

Thank you again for reading. I trust you will enjoy and greatly benefit from the teachings.

1

SOCIAL MEDIA ADVICE

Before we take a deep bite into social media marketing, let's start with the fundamentals of what social media actually is. A social media website or app is any website or any app that meets two criterions. Firstly, it allows its users to share content. Normally the vast majority of this content will be text-based comments, images and videos – but it might also refer to platform specific content for more specialized platforms. Secondly, any social media sites will provide social networking – allowing their users to talk to and interact with other users.

Above and beyond the basic criteria for what defines social media, there are also other patterns that most social media employ. Social media websites usually provide their users with a profile page, where users can demonstrate their identity by photos, comments and personal information (to various levels of security). Additionally, many social media websites will provide their users with a 'feed' which is a stream of content that other users have posted. On top of this, social media platforms typically have a follow/friend/subscribe system which allows a user to link to another user to a greater extent – such as receiving their content in their feed or allowing greater inter-user privileges. Finally, many social media websites also have sharing and voting systems, which allow popular content to be recognized and spread across the website.

With this groundwork established, let's move on to what principles matter to you as a business owner or entrepreneur.

The world of social media relies on the principle of interconnectivity. Connections to other people, the news and our hobbies and interests are the foundation of every social media website out there. Furthermore social media websites are not an island – they rely on spreading and connecting to other social media platforms and hubs.

Whenever you generate internet traffic and buzz through one platform you must learn to aptly direct your traffic to your other social media platforms and to your businesses website. This is one of the key secrets of social media domination – reaching out through multiple websites then consolidating all the attention you have gathered by linking all your viewers to your other platforms. Every large social media websites will have buttons and other inbuilt media to help you promote interconnectivity between platforms.

Ultimately, the point to take home here is that whatever social media campaign you want to start must be cross-platform. Do not take the easy route and stick to the social media website that you are most familiar with, but rather stretch your muscles and spread your message as far as the internet can take you. In this book, a focus will be placed upon five of the largest social media websites; Facebook, Twitter, YouTube, Instagram and LinkedIn, but there are also other popular candidates to bear in mind, such as Bebo and Wordpress.

However, on the same note, it is important not to commit your social media campaign beyond your means and resources. If you cannot devote the love and attention to regularly producing high quality content on a social media website, then you will not reap the benefits that platform can provide. Focus your resources on as many platforms as you can manage. Ideally you should be posting on most platforms at least 2-3 times per week, if not once a day. If you cannot manage this leisurely pace, consider whether you have the time and commitment to use social media for your business.

There are several considerations you should take in to account in regards to the type of content you produce, although the optimal content will vary between social media platforms.

Generally speaking, you want a high proportion of

your content to be image or video based. People are lazy and often use social media sites as a method of mindless distraction or entertainment.

They will not often give your social media campaign much attention unless you either pry it from their unwilling eyes or subtly lure them to your efforts. Text based messages unaccompanied by visuals have been demonstrated to be far less effective at captivating your audience, especially long, wordy text posts. All experienced social media marketers will be using images and videos to grab the attention of social media users and from in a very literal way, your content will be eclipsed by all the flashy images and videos that other users are exploiting. If you can't beat them, join them.

If you do have a lengthy, written post or article you need to share, instead of burdening your social media followers by posting it on their feed, host the post or article on a blog or website. By doing this you can use short, snappy social media posts to advertise those sources of your post or article – using a nice, attention-capturing image or video to gather interest. This is almost guaranteed to be more effective.

Additionally, your content must be high quality. This should go without saying, but too many businesses and advertisers cannot see the forest for the trees when it comes to their social media campaigns. People do not go on Facebook or Twitter to buy products. Spamming their social media feed with adverts and laborious business messages will simply repel any users you might have.

Instead, social media websites are best used as means to generate interest and awareness for your brand and business. They provide a hub where people can go to learn more about you, as well as a tool to engage your customers by providing interesting and entertaining content. There is nothing inherently wrong with advertising a few discounts or offers, but if you go too far, no-one will notice you. In this case, less is more.

On the note of brand awareness, you must always enter a social media campaign with explicit goals envisioned. You must know what kind of message and image for your business you are trying to communicate and who you are trying to communicate it to. You must only convey content that is conducive to your message and make an effort to target the consumers that have a high interest in your product, and thus have the highest likelihood of making a purchase.

Branding through social media is difficult, but nearly every social media website will provide a variety of tools to businesses using their platform. Not only will most social media websites contain a regularly updated blog or feed of tips designed for businesses using their platforms, but they will also provide applications and programs to help you track your user engagement, your page views, your traffic and so on. If you are serious about maximizing the potential of your social media campaign, subscribing to these educational feeds and mastering the inbuilt business tools is essential to success.

Although social media platforms tend to share similar features and partake in similar trends, each platform is still its own creature that needs to be considered in its own entity. To become a social media tycoon you will need to learn the individual features of each social media platform – what each platform specializes in, the strengths and weaknesses of each platform and how to best use each medium for your own purpose. The five most prolific platforms will be explored in this book: Facebook, Twitter, Youtube, LinkedIn and Instagram.

2

FACEBOOK

There are many words that could be used to describe just how big Facebook is, but few could do justice to the 1012 million *daily* users and the 1.52 billion monthly users of Facebook. World population is estimated to be approximately 7.3 billion people. If you do the math, almost one fifth of the earth's entire population is using Facebook every month. It's simply mind-blowing.

Hype aside, Facebook has many features that you need to become intimate with if you want to use it for your business. As a platform, Facebook is rather more diverse than its peers such as Twitter and Instagram. Twitter focuses on bite-size tweets with a helping of image and video content, while Instagram thrives on aesthetically well-ordered photographs and less text. Facebook is more of a jack-of-all trades – though images and video content are well received and most comments are short, Facebook also contains a more sophisticated like system, support for longer textual comments and boasts a greater amount of embedded apps and games than its competitors.

In terms of what this means for your business, there

are a few points to be made. The 'like' and 'share' system is a fantastic tool for businesses once all of its potential is reached. Facebook provides tools in which businesses can promote offers and discounts through the like and share tools, such as lottery-type systems, where everyone who likes a comment has a chance to win a prize. Additionally there are code-based discount systems, where liking and sharing content can give away codes that provide discounts for companies' products. These systems are particularly effective at encouraging engagement and increasing popularity, which can result in greater recognition of your brand.

Similarly, the like system is also great way of interacting with your social media followers. Post content asking your followers business relevant questions and tell them to like the content if they agree – you can use this to get quick, widespread consumer opinions on products you are testing or design decisions you need to make.

Another advantage of Facebook is that it offers the widest range of tools and control options for its users and is also supported by many third-party auxiliary websites that can add color to your Facebook profile and content. There are systems such as Facebook scheduler, which allows you to systematically organize content to be posted at certain times. There are also Facebook plugins and Facebook website embedding, which allow you to connect your business website and your Facebook profile more intimately than other platforms. If you want to make the most of Facebook, visit the *Facebook Business* page (see Links Discussed section), which will take you through all the resources Facebook offers.

As the most powerful and influential of all the social media platforms, Facebook also offers the largest selection of paid advertising options (Pay-Per Click, Pay-Per Impression, Cost-Per Click etc.)

The above mentioned features have a variety of different advertising and scheduling options and require a more thorough investigation beyond the scope of this book to really take advantage of the myriad of marketing potential Facebook offers.

For further exploration of the Facebook marketing platform please see *The 25 Best Strategies on Using Facebook for Advertising, Business and Making Money Online* by Kenneth Lewis, or for an even more in-depth analysis and more advanced strategies, please refer to *Facebook Marketing: How to Use Facebook for Effective Internet Marketing and Social Media Success* in the Excerpt preview section of this book, or by viewing the various complete editions of the publication.

3

TWITTER

Twitter is one of the most prominent of social media sites. It boasts approximately 300 million monthly members, with a huge proportion of those users belonging to a western audience. The marketing potential is huge.

However before you delve into marketing, you need to understand the basics of Twitter and how it differentiates itself from other social media platforms. Firstly, twitter is based on *tweets* posted by its users, which are text messages equal to or less than 140 characters long. Twitter users can follow other users to access their tweets in their homepage feed. Additionally, you can also check a user's profile page to read all their tweets.

Secondly, an essential part of twitter is its usage of hashtags. Several social media sites employ hashtags, but it was Twitter that popularized the hashtag and it is on Twitter that the hashtag is one of the most important features. By adding a '#topic' hashtag to a tweet, such as #fashion or #soccer, you either create a new hashtag, or you add to the pool of tweets about that hashtag. Anyone who searches for that hashtag will be directed to all the tweets using that hashtag. Hashtags are added to the end of a tweet. Creating a unique hashtag or embedding trending relevant hashtags into your tweets is crucial to reaching your audience.

Similarly, the @ feature can be used to link other twitter users in a comparable way. Whenever someone tweets a message with an *@username* tag in their post, the user mentioned will receive a message notifying them of that tweet. This is a fantastic method for making particular users aware of you, by mentioning them. However, at the same time, be mindful not to be invasive. Simply highlighting random uninterested twitter users will be useless, the @ feature should be used to draw attention to trends and relevant user profiles.

One of the ways in which Twitter differentiates itself from other social media websites is that Twitter focuses on *mircroblogging*. The overwhelmingly vast majority of tweets are 1-2 sentences in length. You will need to learn how to tailor your business messages to this size; otherwise they will appear clunky and be ineffectual. Furthermore, as previously discussed in the general advice chapter, these tweets cannot appear to be pure marketing or they will be uninteresting to your followers.

Learning how to tweet messages and promote your business in 1-2 sentences whilst still being noncorporate and engaging is an art. There are no hard rules on how to achieve this, but there are several popular and well-received methods. When promoting your products or services, focus on the benefits and advantages of whatever you are promoting, rather than their existence.

If you can attract followers by offering ways in which you can offer them value and genuinely contribute to their lives, your efforts are more likely to resonate with your audience. Additionally, interact and converse with your Twitter users. Respond to comments and answer potential questions.

Twitter is particularly useful for this type of interaction, as Twitter enforces quick, small communications, which allows you to reach many individuals without being overwhelmed. The Twitter aesthetic is simply designed more effectively for having public conversations with many people better than most other social media websites.

Twitter is also a fantastic platform to create a social media campaign that requires slightly less effort than other social media websites. This isn't the same as saying that you can get away with low quality content, but by its very nature, Twitter marketing tends to require less time and effort for the amount of impact it can generate. Tweets are quick and easy and you can often produce a quality tweet off the top of your head.

Unlike Facebook, which filters its users feed's, only allowing the most relevant and interesting content to pass, everyone who follows you will also see all your Tweets, resulting in slightly less competition.

4

YOUTUBE

As a platform, YouTube focuses almost entirely on video content. Individuals can comment on videos and connect to other users, but these services are far less streamlined then the same services offered on other platforms. However, YouTube generally provides better quality video uploading, an easier method of video creation and organization then other platforms as well as a powerful search function (it is, after all, owned by Google).

YouTube comes with its unique facets. By its very nature, all YouTube content you produce will have to be video based, but generally speaking, you can produce content at a slower pace then other platforms (such as a new video once per week, as opposed to every day). This is because your content doesn't compete directly with other content in such as fast-flowing feed like Twitter or Facebook, so it is less likely to be ignored. Additionally because the search engine embedded in YouTube is so strong it allows people to find you, providing they want to.

Owing to this, focus on producing extremely high-quality content for your YouTube channel.

Brainstorm a unique, engaging idea for a video and take the necessary time to get that video to be as high quality as it can possibly be.

Another aspect of YouTube that needs consideration is the partnership system. Typically most social media websites allow businesses to pay for advertisement, which will appear on a user's feed (or before they watch video content). However, providing your video receives enough viewership, you can enter a partnership with YouTube where they will pay you a flat amount per 1000 views. Generally speaking, this will not amount to much unless your content goes viral, but the possibility of generating income from your videos is still worth recognizing– many individuals do make a rather comfortable living by making popular YouTube videos.

As a final consideration, when using YouTube, place careful thought into your video titles and the possible keywords used in your video description. As YouTube is search-engine based, search engine optimization techniques are especially relevant. Always exploit the keywords you think people will be searching for to maximize your viewership.

5

INSTAGRAM

Instagram is a social media website owned by Facebook and focuses largely on image and photo-based content (although all the usual social media services are available too). Although Instagram can be accessed through the internet via regular desktop or laptop use, the majority of Instagram users are from the Instagram app via mobile, as the service provides easy but advanced ways to turn a mobile phone picture into Instagram content.

As with the other social media websites, the nature of Instagram provides its own challenges and rewards. You must master the art of taking good photos, as Instagram content is predominantly photo-based. If your photos are unattractive or non-aesthetic they will not generate any buzz – pictures should be crisp, bright and taken from an excellent angle. Therefore if you are not a skilled photographer to begin with, try to take multiple photos first and post the best one, or use third-party tools and software to augment your photo-taking skills.

Similarly, whatever you are taking a photo of should be striking to begin with. Obviously an interesting photo is always better than a dull one, but for Instagram where photos are so ubiquitous and photos are often viewed in a sea of other images, your picture really must stand-out.

Additionally, Instagram is a great way to promote the human, relatable aspect of your business. It is wise for any businesses to promote a down-to-earth attitude that will resonate with their customers. This most often translates to focusing on 'behind-the-scenes' and the story-based aspect of the people who work for you and your company, or what they are doing. For Instagram - where photos from mobiles are the life source of its content and mobile photos can be taken anywhere, anytime - this provides a compelling way to spontaneously capture real-life action and give a more genuine behind-the-scene vibe. Be in the moment and impulsive with your Instagram content, opportunistically posting moments from your business that strike you.

Finally, it is worth noting that, Instagram, like Twitter, also focuses heavily on hashtags. Therefore, whenever you post picture content ensure that you have a relevant hashtag to add in your comment – this could be a hashtag unique to your brand but also any hashtag that is relevant, trending or consistently popular.

6

LINKEDIN

Despite being one of the social media titans, LinkedIn provides a rather different service from the four previous platforms mentioned. Whereas Twitter, Facebook, YouTube and Instagram allow companies to focus heavily on business to consumer interaction, LinkedIn specializes in business to business and business to employee interactions. LinkedIn literally provides a professional service. Whilst business people are naturally consumers as well, your approach to LinkedIn will still need to be entirely different to that of the previous platforms.

Firstly, LinkedIn allows you to promote a more corporate image and focuses more heavily on directly marketing and advertising *yourself*. Write about the products and services you provide in a professional business-style tone where the actions and initiatives you have taken appear in a positive light. Similarly, any products or services you offer should also be shown to provide value, reflected in you advertising and marketing descriptions as well.

Have your employees to make LinkedIn profiles. Even though we have already established how

LinkedIn is unique in the social media family, interconnectivity is still written in its genes. The more employees that are associated with your business via LinkedIn, the more avenues LinkedIn users have to find you and the further your impact will make.

In addition to this, directly but politely ask your customers and followers to leave reviews on LinkedIn. Any positive reviews that your customers provide will add up over time and will contribute to developing a potent, visible reputation for future customers who browse your LinkedIn company profile. Remember though – you have to *ask*.

Finally, you will still need to produce content for your LinkedIn page on occasion. This content can be quite different from your regular social media content, whose focus is usually on being entertaining and interesting, but in a very quick and easy way. In contrast, LinkedIn provides a portal for you to post your more meaningful – perhaps more 'professional' - content such as articles, educational material and a statistical review of your business.

Generally speaking, people browse your LinkedIn profile because they have a greater inherent interest in your business or company, rather than just an interest in the witty content you produce. It logically follows these individuals will be more engaged in actual content about your business and willing to take the time and effort to read more serious content.

Nonetheless, this doesn't provide an excuse for dry, boring content. Find the middle ground between factual and informative but appealing and readable.

As previously implied, LinkedIn is also an opportunity for more direct marketing. Feel free to post discounts, company updates and other offers fairly regularly. People have connected to you because they are interested in your particular business; therefore they are likely be interested in the types of products or services your business offers as well. This being said, do not spam or harass your followers. Spamming your customers will simply turn people away. Highlight your appealing, high-value offers to attract followers rather than low-effort, non-genuine 'deals'.

Other LinkedIn specific tips include applying a greater level of effort towards your profile page. For all social media platforms, your profile page should always be customized and well-designed, but beyond that it is mostly a means to re-direct traffic to other sources and promote brand identity. Whilst these factors remain true for LinkedIn, people using LinkedIn will be specifically searching for companies and businesses they might want to use and connect with.

Owing to this, your profile needs to be expertly crafted. Fill your headlines and summaries with key words and ensure that you appear well-dressed and professional in your profile picture. Fill your summaries with a breakdown of what your business does and your targets, goals and philosophy. This is your first impression to potential businesses partners. You will need to look the part and provide all the information potential network connections will need to asses you.

7

LINKS DISCUSSED

Here are the links to the business pages of the various social media websites, as well as the educational content these websites produce to help you become familiar with them.

Facebook

facebook.com/business

facebook.com/Facebook Marketing

Twitter

business.twitter.com

twitter.com/TwitterSmallBiz

YouTube (owned by and connected to Google)

google.com/business

Google Small Business:
youtube.com/user/GoogleBusiness

LinkedIn

business.linkedin.com/marketing-solutions/company-pages/get-started

Instagram

business.instagram.com

blog.business.instagram.com

CONCLUSION

I trust this book was able to help you gain a better understanding of the various social media platforms and develop a broader perspective on the importance of the interconnectivity of online marketing.

Somewhere along the way, social media metamorphosed from a simple system designed to connect friends, families and acquaintances to the greatest business and marketing opportunity of the 21st century. Even more impressively, this juxtaposition of consumer and business manages to be mutually beneficial, as long as the businesses involved know how to play the social media game.

Businesses need to produce content that is out of the ordinary. The need to be attention-grabbing, exciting content producers that are novel enough to be worth following, but not yet bothersome enough to be rejected, is indeed a fine art. When small marketing mishaps can go viral and ruin the reputation of a company, businesses are on a tightrope with no safety nets.

Even more challenging is coming to terms with the different social media platforms and their delicate intricacies. Five years ago, few businesses could have honestly admitted to have a Twitter or Facebook account, and fewer still could give you the reasons to embrace one platform over another. Fast forward five years and your marketing strategy is antiquated if you are not working several social media accounts and not familiar with why you are doing so.

You are now acquainted with all the social media marketing 101. We began by having a crash course on businesses and social media, defining what constitutes a social media platform and general tricks of the trade when using them to market. You now know the importance of interconnectivity, the importance of high-quality content (and what that means) as well as understanding the need to manage your brand.

We then jumped into the finer nuances of various social media platforms. Using five of the largest platforms as examples (Facebook, Twitter, YouTube, Instagram and LinkedIn) we explored what makes each platform special. For each platform we discussed how to transform the unique features of each website into potential marketing success.

You now have the education and tools to launch your social media marketing campaign - if you haven't done so already - and re-invigorate and improve upon any of your existing efforts. Social media is a constantly evolving beast, but by virtue of this guide you now have all the tools you need to succeed in the continually progressing domain of social media marketing.

SHARE YOUR EXPERIENCE

Finally, if you enjoyed or benefited from this book then I would like to ask you for a favor:

Would you be kind enough to leave a review for this book on Amazon?

It would be greatly appreciated!

Thank you, and best of luck on all your social media marketing endeavors!

BONUS EXCERPT

FACEBOOK MARKETING:
How to Use Facebook for
Effective Internet Marketing and
Social Media Success

Facebook is a colossal entity with almost 1 billion daily users interacting with each other and checking their newsfeed for updates about the world. With so many people choosing to access Facebook every day, it is no wonder that it has become one of the greatest marketing assets of this decade.

Facebook actively encourages advertisement efforts on their website and other business relations, providing an abundance of tools and systems for both small and large businesses. However, trying to learn how to market through Facebook poses a steep learning curve. Although a few tips and tricks from tried and tested internet marketing guides are applicable, Facebook needs to be tackled as its own creature, with its own rules.

You need to thoroughly understand how Facebook works on a very fundamental level. This includes topics such as how Facebook determines what content is presented through the newsfeed and the underlying concept of the 'reach' and of organic content.

Your knowledge must also extend to the labyrinthine system of paid advertising and marketing. You need to appreciate the different between a boosted post, a paid advertisement and all the different decisions you should have to make, should you choose to employ either. It is also critical to know how the auction and bidding systems work; the underlying mechanism which determines the cost and charges associated with advertising on Facebook.

This, however, doesn't even cover the tip of the iceberg. You also need to be intimate with the different Facebook business objective goals and the different audiences you can target via all the options Facebook provides. There are the various pricing schemes you can chose, say as pay-per-click, pay-per-impression and optimized pay-per-click that you cannot market without. Additionally, you need to understand the three-part campaign structure of Facebook advertising and the tools offered to manage advertising, such as the power editor.

With these fundamentals covered in the initial chapter, you can then begin to stretch your marketing muscles with Facebook Insights, which presents an entire world of marketing information for you to analyze. If you want to know how many more people liked your content in the past 24 hours, or what your potential reach could be, Facebook Insights is going to be your best friend. Even if you remain mere associates, you need to appreciate Facebook Insights for what the feedback and power it offers you to refine and improve your marketing efforts.

With Facebook Insights now firmly understood, you can start to really bring your marketing tactics to the next level with more advanced strategies. If you are naïve about dark posting or if you think pixels are just to do with your screen resolution, then the strategies within this book will give you an enlightening wake-up call. Learn how to target niche audiences, improve conversions, create custom audiences and re-target missed buyers with the sophisticated and complex opportunities Facebook presents.

With your marketing expertise now reaching intimidating levels, you will then be presented with all the various resources that you can utilize to give yourself the Facebook marketing edge. Find out where you can access Facebook's free 34 part marketing e-learning course, or where you should be waiting to hear the latest Facebook news and updates.

With your Facebook mastery established, you must be prudent to stay on top of the game by keeping up to date with all the changes and updates Facebook is developing for release in the near future. Facebook puts light itself to shame with just how fast it rushes ahead.

If you simply sit on the knowledge of established techniques without taking the initiative to keep your knowledge fresh, then you will soon find yourself a Facebook novice once more. Learn about highly anticipated changes, such as Facebook Reactions, Facebook Immersive ads and Facebook Connectivity - changes that may shake the foundations of the current Facebook marketing platform we know today.

Chapter 1: Facebook 'Organic' Reach

Originally, all content a user posted on Facebook would be seen by their followers on their news feeds. However, as Facebook became more popular and the average user subscribed to more content, Facebook implemented a system to filter and restrict the amount of content users see. Now, only a portion of content gets seen by followers, which prevents users from feeling overwhelmed as well as protect them viewing from diluted, poor content – or rather content that they simply will not be interested in. This system is called 'Facebook Reach' and refers to how far and how much penetration (i.e reach) your Facebook content achieves.

Facebook reach deals with 'organic' content. Organic refers to content that is naturally filtered through search engine and social media engines. This organic content is then ranked and filtered according to its quality, and thus generates a certain amount of exposure or traffic based on the ranking it receives.

Although most marketers will also employ Facebook Boost and Facebook Paid Advertising, Facebook Reach is where every internet marketer will want to start. If you learn to play the game and abide by the rules, you can still ensure a high amount of your organic content reaches your desired audience. Furthermore, Facebook Reach is free and is a great way for internet marketers to test the shallow waters before they dive in to the deep end.

Facebook Reach uses an algorithm to filter content and decide whether that content is worth your follower's time. The original algorithm, called 'Edgerank' uses three factors (affinity, edge weight and time decay.

Affinity, Weight and Time Decay

Affinity refers to how well two users are known to each other, and how interconnected their lives are. If two users frequently interact across Facebook, frequently tag each other or belong to many of the same groups and share many of the same friends, than these users will have high affinity. Affinity takes into account clicking on user content, liking, commenting, tagging, sharing and friend-ing as measures of connectedness.

It is important to note that affinity is asymmetrical; user A can have a high affinity towards user B without user B having high affinity towards user A.

Additionally, each action you perform on Facebook has a different 'edge weight'. Simply put, certain actions are considered more important and more telling than others. It is easy and non-committal to like or share content. Commenting however, implies a closer relationship between two users. At the very least, it signals more effort. Owing to this, commenting has a higher edge weight than liking and will be more influential in Facebook Edgerank.

Edge weight is believed to be contextual in the sense that certain actions will be weighted higher or lower depending on the users involved, rather than having a static value. If a user prefers to share content, but rarely tends to comment, then sharing content might receive a higher edge rank for this particular user, based upon that particular Facebook habit.

To read the rest of *Facebook Marketing*, visit Amazon.com and search 'Facebook Kenneth Lewis'.

OTHER WORKS BY KENNETH LEWIS

Facebook Marketing (Advanced): How to Use Facebook for Effective Internet Marketing and Social Media Success

Facebook Marketing: The 25 Best Strategies on Using Facebook for Advertising, Business and Making Money Online

Passive Income: Make Money Online and Achieve Financial Freedom - How To Make $500 - $12 K with only $50

The Procrastination Cure: Overcome Procrastination, Be Productive and Learn Time Management Strategies for Life

Interview and Get Any Job You Want: Employment Techniques and How to Answer Toughest Interview Questions

All books are available in e-book format, and many are also available in audio-book and paperback format as well. Visit Amazon.com to view available editions.

ABOUT THE AUTHOR

For over thirty years Kenneth has been active in the marketing and business force, working for various companies as well as pursuing his own independent projects. He has most recently began publishing introductory books on internet marketing and other various aspects of social media as a way to share his passion and interests with those who are new to these domains.

His books aim to be practical, easy to understand and follow. His books also serve as reference guides to those who are already somewhat familiar with the online marketing sector.

In his spare time, Kenneth enjoys golfing, fishing, and spending time with his family at their lake house. Kenneth is also an avid cook and enjoys experimenting with different recipes.

www.ingramcontent.com/pod-product-compliance
Lightning Source LLC
Chambersburg PA
CBHW021003180526
45163CB00005B/1868